ASTROLOGY IN PREDICTING WEATHER AND EARTHQUAKES

AF215291

Astrology in Predicting Weather and Earthquakes

DR. B. V. RAMAN

MOTILAL BANARSIDASS
INTERNATIONAL
DELHI

Reprint Edition : Delhi, 2024
First Edition : 1992

© MOTILAL BANARSIDASS INTERNATIONAL
All Rights Reserved

ISBN : 978-81-19394-51-7

Also available at
MOTILAL BANARSIDASS INTERNATIONAL

H. O. : 41 U.A. Bungalow Road, (Back Lane)Jawahar Nagar, Delhi - 110 007
4261 (basement) Lane #3,Ansari Road, Darya Ganj, New Delhi - 110 002
203 Royapettah High Road, Mylapore, Chennai - 600 004
12/1A, 2nd Floor, Bankim Chatterjee Street, Kolkata - 700 073
Stockist : Motilal Books, Ashok Rajpath, Near Kali Mandir, Patna - 800 004

No part of this book may be reproduced in any form or by any
electronic or mechanical means including information storage and retrieval
systems without permission in writing from the publishers, excepts by a
reviewer who may quote brief passages in a review.

Printed in India
MOTILAL BANARSIDASS INTERNATIONAL

Contents

Foreword

This small volume on weather and earthquake prediction is perhaps the only work that explores Nature's moods from the astrological angle. I was able to compile this work in 1992 showcasing the *Father of Modern Astrology* Dr. B.V.Raman's seminal work in the area of seismic disasters and weather vagaries drawing from his editorials in the now defunct *The Astrological Magazine.*

Compared to the performance of the Seismology Department and the Meteorological Department, astrology has a far far better record. Many of the major earthquakes between the late 1960's and the 1990's were anticipated both date-wise and site-wise months in advance by Dr.Raman based on astrological factors identified by him and drawn from classical works on astrology.

The Government of India would be doing yeoman service to the world and humanity at large if it only incorporated the astrological factors in the working of its Earthquake and Weather related departments which as everyone knows have a miserable record of never forecasting seismic disasters but only explaining their magnitude only after they have struck and resulted in heavy loss of human lives and destruction of crores of rupees worth of property.

I am sure that some day the official seismologist and meteorologist will take note of the guidelines in this slender volume and improve thereby their own performance in their respective fields of work.

Out of print for over two decades after Dr.Raman's demise in December 1998, this volume is now brought out by Mr. J.P. Jain and Mr.Abhishek Jain of Messrs. Motilal Banarasidaas International to whom I express my gratitude. I must also thank them for making this invaluable work available to future generations as otherwise It would have been lost to posterity.

Bangalore   **Gayatri Devi Vasudev**
July 10, 2024

Preface

Putting together my father Dr. B. V. Raman's pioneering work in forecasting earthquakes through astrology has been an eye opening experience. Going through the editorials of *The Astrological Magazine*, one came across many brilliant predictions proved to veracity with amazing but tragic precision. These predictions stand in strong contrast to the dismal forecasts of seismologists.

The Seismology Department maintained at a considerable cost by the government has done precious little to justify its existence. On the other hand, the government's supine ignorance to the tremendous potential of astrology is indigestible, especially since these fore-warnings can save countless lives and suffering.

The astrological methods are, by and large, fairly reliable and accurate. However, much work yet remains to be done in locating more precisely the site of the occurrence of an earthquake. But where individual effort and resources are the only means as has been the case with my father, this stupendous task remains difficult.

Mr. S. K. Kelkar, a well-known astrologer of Pune, has been working on this aspect of earthquakes and many of his forecasts have been fulfilled.

I appeal to all right thinking persons, whether in positions of authority in the government or in scientific bodies, to be broad-minded enough to set aside their prejudices (which are but a hangover of the colonial days when a massive inferiority complex was insidiously injected into the Indian psyche) to study the astrological clues Dr. Raman has collected as a result of decades of study of the science of astrology and to integrate these clues into their own methods to pinpoint occurrences of earthquakes.

I am confident that my father's dedicated work in asteroseismology, which he has pursued with a missionary zeal, will come to fruition. That, some day some thinkers capable of feeling for humanity will apply it with success, assuaging thereby the suffering an earthquake invariably leaves behind in its trail.

Simple ground rules have been listed in this book. These have been culled from different editorials on earthquakes written by my father in the course of the last five decades. Anyone with a little knowledge of astrology and general science can use these rules to forecast earthquakes with considerable success. This in itself is a great achievement when the score of the official seismologist is just .01 per cent or even less.

Astrology also provides much information on weather forecasting, especially of rainfall. Heavy, scanty and delayed rains can all be indicated fairly accurately. Long-range forecasting of weather has also been elaborately dealt with in classical works which has also been highlighted in this book. Short-term forecasts of a few hours, one day and even a week can be made accurately. The only person I have come across in India, with a bent of mind for research in the field of forecasting weather on the basis of astrology, as developed by ancient seers and in the light of a modern approach to the subject, is Mr. K. N. Rao, L.A.A.S. (Retd.). In fact several of his forecasts on weather based on astrology have been fulfilled, while those of the meteorologists have failed.

The information and guidelines that astrology provides in weather forecasting can be of great consequence in planning all kinds of activities. I hope those genuinely interested in unlocking the secrets of nature will seriously study the basic astrological information *vis-a-vis* earthquakes and weather provided in these pages and employ it for the benefit of mankind for which the science of astrology was founded by the great rishis of India.

Bengaluru   **Gayatri Devi Vasudev**
18-6-1992

Section 1

Astrology in Weather Prediction

Heavy Rainfall and Sunspot Maxima

Some years ago, on a Friday, the weather experts were expecting thunderstorms over the north-western region of India. But hell broke loose in Delhi in the shape of a tornado—hailstones, the size of golf balls accompanied by violent rain and strong currents of wind lifting people and scooters into the air, dragging buses across the road and uprooting everything in sight, from trees to telegraph posts, resulting in hundreds of men and women ending up in the emergency wards of Delhi's major hospitals. The weathermen did not predict this.

Earlier in 1977, life in large parts of coastal Andhra Pradesh came to a standstill on 11 November. A cyclone of tremendous intensity hit the coast, killing over 20,000 people and destroying property, crops and livestock worth an estimated three billion rupees. The Meteorological Department had failed again.

The Meteorology Institute had previously forecast the possibility of rain over Java at the time of the eclipse of 11th June, 1983. But the skies were clear and 11th June passed off without a drop of rain.

There is a certain statutory obligation resting squarely on the scientific community to make correct forecasts. Ironically, the Meteorological Department on which crores of rupees are being lavished to maintain an army of officials simply issues bulletins not worth the paper on which they are written.

Research studies conducted in the West indicate that periods of very heavy rainfall also coincide with sunspot maxima. Floodings of the Nile in Egypt also follow the solar cycle, being greatest at sunspot maxima. All things considered it is reasonable to conclude that at such times (*viz.*, sunspot maxima) there is a higher rainfall over the Earth and there are greater number of storms in the tropical regions. Moreover, the general circulation of the atmosphere is more violent which makes the temperature over the globe slightly lower than the normal average. Meteorological changes are also related to geo-magnetic storms which, in turn, depend on changes taking place in the Sun. In any case, there is enough evidence to establish that there is a correlation between solar and terrestrial meteorological phenomena.

The cause of the sunspot cycle, which is still a mystery, appears to synchronise with the period of Jupiter's orbit around the Sun. Just as the Sun and the Moon raise tides in the oceans and the atmosphere of the Earth, and even in the solid Earth itself, so does the gravity of the planets raise tides on the surface of the Sun.

2,000 years ago, the great Varahamihira dealt with the question of sunspots and their effects on the Earth, fairly exhaustively at a time when the western countries perhaps did not know whether the Sun rose in the east or the west. In fact, he also said that the appearance of these spots would bring thunderbolts, Earthquakes and such unusual phenomena boding calamity.

It has been noticed even by the western scientists that every 11 years or so there are great bursts of solar activity. During the maximum periods there is an acceleration of the 'Earth's heartbeats' causing, as we shall see in Section 2, a larger number of Earthquakes, a phenomenon which as yet no scientist has been able to explain fully but which is an indisputable fact. It has also been found that sunspots cause the eruption of violent winds releasing charged corpuscles which cause terrestrial magnetic storms.

It is no more a question of superstition or doubtful assumption that there exists a connection between solar activity and the climate and weather on Earth. Even as early as 1880, the French astronomer Camille Flammarian wrote in Popular Astronomy that "in our French climates, cold rainy years and floods coincide with calm periods of the Sun when there are no eruptions and spots, whereas arid and sultry years coincide with periods of the most intense solar activity."

It looks as though what Varahamihira said years ago, echoed when the Russian scientist A.V. Dyakov observed "the number of the spots, their size, shape and location on the Sun disc have to be carefully noted" for weather forecasting. In fact Varahamihira says that if there should appear in the Sun's disc, spots in the form of a stick, it portends the death of the sovereign; if it appears like a headless body there will be outbreak of diseases; if the form is that of the Keelaka (or wedge) there will be famine.

दन्डे नरेन्द्र मृत्युः व्याधिभयस्यात् कबन्ध संस्थाने ।
दुर्भिक्षं कीलके अर्कस्थें ॥

Again Dyakov says that should the spots assume jagged outlines and approach the centre of the solar disc or cross the equator, we may well expect meteorological cataclysms on the Earth.

Let us make it clear that weather can be forecast with considerable accuracy only on the basis of observing processes taking place on the Sun, which in their turn, are correlated to certain planetary juxtapositions.

Looking at the planetary positions on cyclonic days, we come across another interesting correspondence which when used in conjunction with sunspot maxima and conventional weather forecasting techniques, can be of tremendous value in predicting future cyclones.

A simple forecast of the weather is very general in scope. It is a simple fact that you cannot forecast a flood in the middle of a desert or a cold wave in the tropics because things like that do not happen within a lifetime but by all means one cannot rule out such a possibility. The forecaster must be familiar with climatology in all of its phases as well as the geography of the land. This is very important.

Effect of Slow Moving Planets

Research has shown that when the planet Jupiter is in perihelion there is a great drought and likewise when in aphelion there is more dampness and cold weather than usual. Changes in the weather are associated with the Sun, the Moon and the planets under certain conditions of positions, either when they act alone or in combination.

Strong positions or aspects of planets leave strong impressions on the weather progressively all over the world. The slower moving planets (especially Jupiter and Saturn) exert a telling influence, because of their slow speed and their great masses for a longer period of time.

The Sun's Influence

The Sun's contact with the planets has its own effects on the weather conditions on Earth.

With Mercury, the weather is given to windy spells along coastal areas and increases the depth of high and low pressure systems.

With Venus, the weather gives rise to an increase in rain or snow.

With Mars, the weather becomes warmer, according to the season.

With Jupiter, the weather becomes dry and sometimes as the season changes, it will bring drought.

With Saturn, the pressure is stagnant over long periods and colder than normal for the season.

With Rahu, the weather is severe for the season and there are local storms during any month as well as the season.

With Ketu, the weather is very changeable, with many changes within a short space of time.

When Mercury and Venus pass the Sun, usually wet and windy weather occurs. The position of the Sun at times of new Moon and season-changes will give the observer a clue as to the type of weather likely during a specified period of time. The position of the Sun in the Nadir in any chart controls the weather over the area for a certain longitude and latitude.

When Mercury Conjuncts Sun

Mercury-conjunct-Sun is the most important aspect to be taken into account when forecasting weather because Mercury itself is a rapid-moving planet and the positions of the conjunctions are very important.

It is generally found that when Mercury and the Sun are in conjunction during the winter, a blizzard or a cold wave occurs.

When Mercury and the Sun are in superior conjunction followed by Mercury's conjunction with or opposition to Mars, and Rahu conjuncts Sun, a fast moving cold wave may be brought about. Temperatures may fall rapidly.

Mercury and Saturn in mutual aspect may keep the area of rising temperatures limited. An aspect of Venus can bring moist warm air and a promise of moderate to heavy rain or even storms or tornadoes.

Important methods have been given by ancient writers for forecasting floods.

They are:

(a) times of pregnancy of clouds;

(b) entry of the Sun into the constellation of Aridra;

(c) the Sun's entry into Capricom:

(d) Rohini, Swati and Ashadha Yogas; and

(e) mutual dispositions of planets and the transit of planets in different Nadis such as *Vatanadi, Amritanadi, Sooryanadi, Jalanadi*, etc.

Using these methods the Hindu astrologers could foretell years of scarcity and plenty, pestilence, Earthquakes, floods, inundations etc.

Mars and Dry Weather

Coming to the planet Mars, it raises the temperature. causing a dryness in the weather, especially when in Aries. If there is persistent drought and scarcity of water, the culprit is again Mars. Mars also causes pestilent and blasting winds accompanied by droughts and lightning emitted from the sky. At sea, there is a likelihood of ships wrecked by the turbulence of winds and strokes of lightning. Mars in conjunction with Jupiter exerts a disturbing effect on the weather, and storms of rain and thunder occur during the rainy season. Thunder, lightning and inundations are the outcome of Saturn-Mars influences.

How the Winds are Influenced

Mercury generates acute, sharp and whipping winds; Venus generates sunny weather consistent with the season; Mars gives rise to energetic watery winds and abnormally hot summers, and Saturn's action is frequently related to chronic cloudy skies and abnormal rainfall.

Lunatics, hysterical or nervous people, neurotics and epileptics are very much under the beams of the Moon and it is a well-known fact that institutions housing such individuals have to be on guard during the Moon's changing phases, and especially during the full Moon. A few years ago the Chief of the New York Fire Department prepared a statistical study of the incidence of fire break-outs. He found, confirming astrological methods, that by far the greatest number of such fires were started at the time of the full Moon.

Planetary Clues to Cyclones

The fury of nature becomes abundantly evident in the grim devastation caused annually by floods in India. The South-West Monsoon period, though usually welcome, causes so much havoc that lakhs of people are rendered homeless and crores of rupees worth of property destroyed. It is estimated that the loss of property in the state of Karnataka alone amounts to about rupees six crores. Damage to crops and property is indeed considerable in the coastal states of Kerala and Tamil Nadu. In the south, the Cauvery has always been benevolent, and it must be beyond comprehension of the high level Committee on floods, why the Cauvery was so wrathful in 1961, that it belied the fond hope of the Committee expressed many years ago: "there was no flood problem on this river." The ancient Chola rulers were certainly more realistic in the interests of the people, when they devised the Grand Anicut, a flood moderator, about a thousand years ago.

The intensity and horror of the tragedy of floods in Poona (now Pune) in 1961 were equally shocking. Heavy rains breached the Panshet and the Khadakvasla dams and the entire city was immersed in water. The devastation caused was perhaps far worse than the official estimate.

In the 1961 Annual of *The Astrological Magazine*, I wrote nearly nine months in advance: "The rainfall will be heavy and the land will be simply inundated with water. During the rainy season, there will be excessive rainfall accompanied with high winds and hailstorms, and severe gales would cause loss of life and property. It is also said that most of the rain will fall in the seas and mountains. The ratio of wind to rain will be three to four units respectively. The crops will be good but just before the time of harvest, there will be much destruction by pests. Most of the rivers in India will be in spate but the flooding of the waters of Ganga, Cauvery and Godavari will cause lot of havoc affecting the safety of large masses of people and cattle."

I was able to anticipate on the basis of the ancient science of Astrology, what Meteorology and its experts could not.

It is a matter of common occurrence that village astrologers are right in a surprisingly high percentage of their weather predictions. Their rules are simple and dispense away with costly apparatus and laboratories. Observation coupled with experience enabled the great sages of India to delve deep into the subject of astro-meteorology which was taken by them as a branch of Astrology because the heavenly bodies, the aspects, the conjunctions etc., are all common to both. Every member of the solar system exerts an important influence by gravitation upon every other and the Sun in particular produces diurnal, annual and other variations in the inclination and declination of the magnetic needle and effects may possibly be produced upon the very mobile atmosphere of the Earth too.

In *Brihat Samhita,* Varahamihira devotes eight chapters to the science of forecasting rain. His thesis is that as "food is the elixir of life and food depends upon rain, it is important to discover the laws of rain carefully". Mihira is so confident that he asserts that "the prediction of an astrologer who pays exclusive attention both day and night, to the indications of rain afforded by the conception of clouds, will come true like the words of a sage."

Modern meteorologists would do well to ponder over Varahamihira's challenge: "What science can possibly excel Astrology, which determines the exact time of rain and by a thorough study of which one gets the power of predicting the past, present and the future even in this Kali Yuga which destroys all good things?"

To determine the amount of rain one may expect during the rainy season, one has to study the conditions of the atmosphere six months earlier. Long-range forecast was a speciality with our ancient astro-meteorologists. According to Garga and other sages, the clouds become pregnant from the day the Moon reaches the constellation of Poorvashadha in the bright half of the lunar month Margasira (Third week of November each year).

The ancient theory that the Moon exercises regulatory control over weather variations has now become an accepted fact of science, thanks to the research of some Australian scientists. While the Moon's varying distance from the Sun, i.e., lunar day or *tithi* is a potent factor in weather changes, there is an overwhelming evidence that the major planets have a powerful influence over atmospheric eventualities.

Research has revealed that about twice as many tropical storms have whirled to hurricane intensity on the three days centered at new Moon and full Moon. Meteorologists in U.S.A. have found what they call an incidence of correlation between years rich in rainfall and Jupiter's movements.

A cyclone of tremendous intensity hit the Andhra Pradesh coast on 19th November, 1977 killing over 20,000 people and destroying property, crops and livestock worth an estimated three billion rupees. It was not, however, totally unexpected. Two days earlier a severe cyclone had hit the neighbouring state of Tamil Nadu and most knew that the storm was heading towards Andhra Pradesh. But two days was not just enough time to prepare to receive the impact of the century's most devastating cyclone. The Meteorological Department had failed again and inspite of the statement of the Government of Andhra Pradesh that the Meteorological Department had given storm warning and precautions had been taken", the people knew who were to be blamed. The statement was a cruel joke and an insult to the suffering people of the state.

Very few newspapers had the courage to point out the inadequate and unscientific attitude of the Meteorological Department of India. Some hoped that with the completion of project Monex and the installation of some more scanners, they would be able to study weather patterns better. It is indeed a sad commentary on the apathy of the general public that crores of rupees have been frittered away by the Meteorological Department with no questions asked and no doubts raised. An example in point is the almost blind installation of scanners on the Andhra Pradesh coast. The department prides itself on the fact that the scanners can follow a cyclonic path up to 400 kms. But with cyclonic speeds being in excess of 100 kms per hour this would give a four-hour warning, hardly time enough to prepare to face a cyclone.

The failure of meteorologists is mainly due to a lack of sufficient scientific open-mindedness which prevents them from considering extra-terrestrial happenings as responsible for weather changes on the Earth.

Meteorological changes are also related to geo-magnetic storms which, in turn, depend on events taking place in the Sun. It is worth noting that in 1957, a year of exceptional solar conditions, the United States had an extremely large number of cyclones.

Disturbances on the Sun affect different parts of the Earth in different ways by producing changes of temperature or pressure, humidity, rainfall and even storms.

The solar wind is a stream of electrically charged particles which blows along the lines of force of the Sun's magnetic field. This is funnelled into the polar regions by the Earth's magnetic field. Once they get into the Earth's upper atmosphere, small particles such as these act as 'seeds' on which crystals of ice are produced. There may be other ways in which solar activity and the solar wind affect the weather. Studies of variations in the solar wind, as measured from the Pioneer Spacecraft, provide another clue. The solar wind is more 'gusty' around the time of maximum solar activity. There is statistical proof that when the Sun is more active, producing flares and spots, the solar wind contains more high-speed streams. And these high-speed streams are very likely to affect the weather on the Earth.

Another piece of direct evidence linking sunspots and the weather comes from records of the occurrences of storms and lightning in the United Kingdom.

Dr. M. F. Stringfellow of the U.K. Electricity Council Research Center has published graphs (Fig. 1) which indicate that the annual lightning incidence (which is a measure of the number of lightning flashes occurring in a given area each year) closely follows the mean sunspot index.

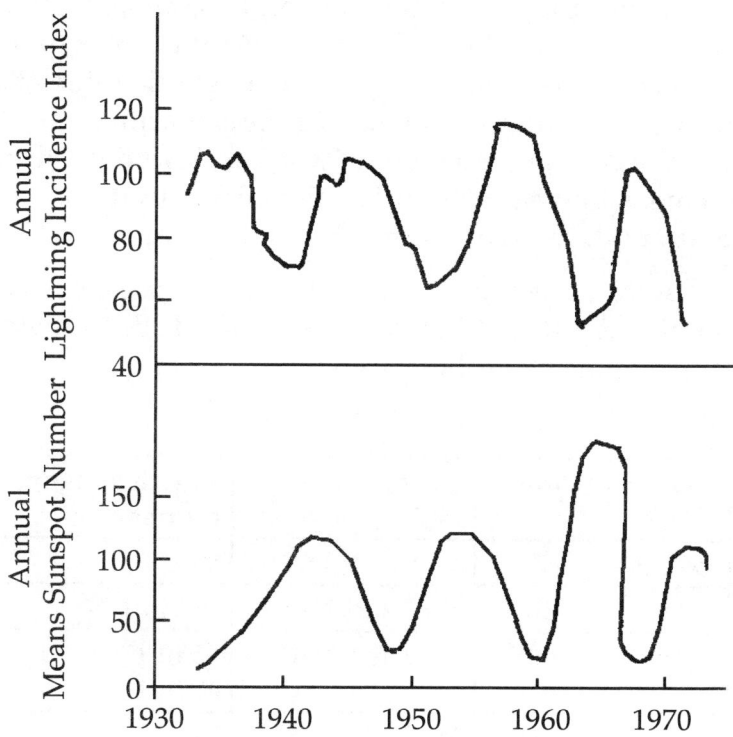

Fig. 1. Top: Annual Lightning Index
(as described previously)

Bottom: Yearly Mean Sunspot Number.
(Dr. M. F. Stringfellow, Nature)

Just as the Sun and the Moon raise tides in the oceans, the atmosphere of the Earth and even in the solid Earth, so does the gravity of the planets raise tides on the surface of the Sun. And the height of the total tide depends on the relative alignments of the planets.

The Earth's magnetic field seems to be linked with the weather. Studies conducted by the U.S. Weather Bureau show a steady increase in magnetic intensity in England, Sweden and Egypt as well as a steady decrease in temperature. At the same time in Mexico, Canada and U.S.A., the magnetic intensity is decreasing and the climate is getting warmer. Sudden changes in magnetic intensity are followed by abrupt changes in weather. And again solar activity has a lot to do with the Earth's magnetic intensity.

A study of some of the most devastating cyclones on the Andhra Pradesh coast (see Table I below) shows that they follow sunspot maxima.

Table I

Year of Cyclone		Sunspot	Zurich sunspot number
April	1752	1750	83
Dec.	1879	1787 and 1788	132 in 1787
Oct.	1800	1802 and 1804	45 in 1802 48 in 1804
May	1832 1839	1830 1837	71 138
Nov.	1879	1870	139
Nov.	1927	1928	78
Oct.	1936	1937	114
Oct.	1949	1947	152
Nov.	1969	1967 and 1968	190 in 1967 185 in 1968

The planetary positions on cyclonic days reveal another interesting correlation. This correlation when used in conjunction with sunspot maxima and conventional weather forecasting techniques can be of tremendous value in predicting future cyclones.

For example, on the day of the 1927 cyclone, there were loose conjunctions between Jupiter and Uranus and between Saturn and Ketu. In 1936, we find a Jupiter-Rahu conjunction. In 1949, there was a Saturn-Ketu conjunction in Virgo, the ruling sign of India. 1969 saw a Saturn-Jupiter opposition and a Rahu-Uranus conjunction, the latter combination aspecting the 12th from Virgo. The 1977 cyclone synchronised with a Jupiter-Rahu square and Saturn in the 12th (loss, death, etc.) from India's ruling sign.

It seems that cyclones on the Andhra Pradesh coast are likely to occur close to periods of sunspot maxima when the planets Jupiter, Saturn, Rahu (Ketu) and Uranus form even loose aspects of Kendra (square) and Samagama (conjunction) between themselves. These indications are strengthened whenever either Virgo or the 12th from it are afflicted.

When a suspected periodicity crops up in observations but cannot be proved, the obvious thing is to find a physical reason why such a period should exist. All things point to the influence of the Sun on the Earth and the influence of relative planetary alignments on the Sun.

Kepler, the great astronomer, to whose laws, even Newton was indebted, for many of his discoveries, struck the correct note when he asserted that "a most unfailing experience of the excitement of sub-lunary natures, by the conjunction and aspects of the planets, has instructed and compelled my unwilling belief." As Dr. Pearce says: "If the meteorologists of the present day will but follow lead of Kepler in meteorology, as Newton did in astronomy, they will constitute meteorology as a predictive science." It is the planetary Yogas—geometrical positions—in respect to themselves, the signs and the constellations that make the weather. The late John O'Neill, Science Editor of The New York *Herald Tribune* stated: "The hypothesis given by the astrologers that forces are transmitted to the Earth without attenuation with increasing distance, and do not vary with respect to the difference in masses of the Sun, Moon and planets on which they originate, was totally inconsistent with the old style Newtonian mechanics; but today is in complete accord with the much more recent Einstein photo-electric theory which demonstrates that the effect on a photon does not diminish with distance, and which has been universally adopted by scientists to supplant the Newtonian mechanics in that field."

Further, "The hypothesis, put forward by the astrologers, that different effects will be produced by different configurations of the heavenly bodies, is entirely consistent with the modern developments in the field of chemistry, in which the properties of substances are stated in terms of the architectural configurations of the atoms within the molecules, and with the theories of the atomic physicists that the properties of the atoms are associated with the orbital architecture of the electrons."

It cannot be a lucky hit that scientist John Nelson has stumbled upon a 'puzzling coincidence' between meteorological facts and astrological assumptions. He found certain planetary arrangements—which in the astrological language are called benefic aspects—are apparently pacifying to the ionosphere. According to Nelson the most severe ionospheric disturbances will come when the "combined influences of Mars, Venus and Mercury are such that all the three are arrayed in positions where there will be a great concentration of planetary influences near Jupiter-Saturn team," and these are correlated to magnetic disturbances on the Earth. As Tice explains: "The Earth and its atmosphere, though intensely charged with electricity, may be perfectly tranquil; until either it encounters an exciting cause in its own orbit, or until it is affected by similar occurrences in Mercury, Venus, Mars and Jupiter, when instantly a spasmodic paroxysm occurs either by Earthquakes and volcanic eruptions on the Earth, by hurricanes, immense rainfall and terrific electric explosions in the atmosphere, or by all combined, synchronous in time and often coincident in place."

"Since magnetic disturbances are but electric disturbances, and since sunspots are synchronous with sudden and violent, electric currents on the Earth, and electric currents are synchronous with oscillations in atmospheric pressure, with rain and windstorms, with hurricanes and with Earthquakes, therefore we know that the bond of union between all these phenomena is electricity. The periodicity of the phenomena is owing to the ebbs and flows of electricity, and the ebbs and flows of electricity in the solar system ensue from the peculiar relations that subsist between the Sun and each planet at its equinoctial and solstitial points."

Prediction of Rain

Astrology can provide reliable rain forecasts. Because of their training and *apriori* considerations, some scientists have a tendency to disregard this fact of great importance that Astrology can be more accurate than meteorology. It must be noted that in Astrology as in other fields of scientific study, the great temptation that exists is the urge to deal with the problem by over-simplifying it. Thus for instance, the western astrologer might stick to the proposition that a certain aspect between two major planets might cause storms. This inference is indeed an over-simplification and not consistent with the techniques employed in Hindu Astrology. The comprehensive methods of weather forecasting are to be found in ancient classics and they should be understood and applied through systematic investigation and research for excellent results.

Science is beginning to indirectly endorse astrological theories. For instance, in 1962, Glen W. Brier of the Massachusetts Institute of Technology announced the discovery of a remarkable correlation between the phases of the Moon and rainfall in U.S.A. Similar results were arrived at independently by E. E. Adderley of the Radiophysics Division of the CSIRO in Australia. When precipitation data were found in terms of the Moon's phases, it was found that heavy rain occurred most frequently about four days after full Moon and reached a secondary peak about four days after new Moon. In other words, the greatest amount of rain fell when the Moon was either 45 or 225 degrees from the Sun. These findings were based on the study of data taken from the U.S. Weather Bureau precipitation statistics covering the period 1900-1949 and dates of maximum rainfall for each calendar month.

When Rain Increases

It should be within the keen observation of a student of Astrology that rain tends to increase when the Moon is at one of its nodes irrespective of its phase. Whether the mechanism involved is gravitational or electrical we do not know. But there is no doubt that a clear correlation exists between the movements of the Moon and variations in quantities of rainfall.

The positions of planets in the north of the celestial equator have a definite influence on the movement of the pressure systems for periods of whole seasons.

When a planet enters Cancer, it will influence the weather more in the northern hemisphere while the southern hemisphere is more influenced when the sign is Capricorn.

How Asterisms Regulate Weather

When the Sun and the Moon are in neutral asterisms there will be winds; when they are in feminine asterisms there will be lightning and phosphorescence; and when the Sun occupies a feminine asterism, and the Moon a masculine asterism, or *vice-versa* there will be rains.

Heavy Rains and When They Occur

At the time of the Sun's ingress into Gemini, if Venus occupies the 2nd or 12th from the rising sign and when at the same time, the Moon occupies a watery Navamsa in any sign, there will be copious rains during the year in question (Aries to Pisces is a year).

When the Sun, the Moon, Mars, Saturn and Rahu cross the watery signs in transit and Mercury, and Venus conjoin a Sthoola Rasi, there will be very heavy rains.

When the Sun, Mercury and Venus occupy the same sign and the same Navamsa, there will be heavy rains. But if these planets occupy the same Rasi (sign) and Navamsa and they happen to be watery signs, the rains will be all the more heavy.

When the Sun occupies an Earthy sign and the Moon, Mercury and Venus occupy watery signs, and at that time if a rainbow is seen in the western side, then also there will be rains in plentiful.

Rainbows in Different Seasons

In Varsha *ritu* (July-August) a rainbow in the eastern side does not give rain.

In the other *ritus* (seasons) a rainbow in the east will bring in rains.

A rainbow in the west during the Varsha *ritu* brings in a downpour.

The Mock Sun and its Effects

When the mock Sun is visible to the north of the Sun's disc, there will be rain; to the south there will be a tempest; and on both sides, a flood will come in. To the top of the Sun's disc means some danger to the king, and below will mean some calamities to the people.

Rain at New Moon Heralds Goods Rains

When it rains on the new Moon days and the days succeeding them (Prathipada days) there will be good rainfall during that bright half of the lunar month.

If it rains on full Moon days and the dark Prathipada (1st lunar date) there will be no rains in the dark half.

In both *Pakshas* (half-lunar months) when it rains during the first 15 *ghatikas* (6 hours) in Dwiteeya (2nd lunar day) and the last 15 *ghatikas* in Prathipada (1st lunar day) there will be copious rains during those *Pakshas* (fortnights).

When it rains only a little on these days, rains will be scarce during those *Pakshas* (fortnights).

If it does not rain then, there will be no rain during that *Paksha* (fortnight).

Direction of Winds and Rainfall

When the winds blow from the north-east in the evening (sandhya) of the full Moon day of Ashadha (July-August) there will be downpour and consequent luxuriant vegetable life during the ensuing year.

Lunar Days and Rainfall

When it rains on the 4th lunar day of the dark half of Ashadha (July-August) on the day ruled by

Poorvabhadra in the same month, there will be luxuriant vegetation during the year ahead.

When the 5th lunar day of the bright half of the lunar month falls on a Sunday (in Ashadha), there will be a little rain.

Weekdays and Rains

If such a day is on a Monday there will be a downpour.

If it is a Tuesday, rains will be fierce. If Wednesday it would bring in a storm.

If a Thursday, general prosperity.

If a Friday, rain and loss; and

If a Saturday, there will be misery everywhere.

Terrible Rains

If the constellation of Rohini coincides with the 10th lunar day (in the month of Ashadha) there will be excessive rains.

The information below is useful in giving long range forecasts which appear to have been a speciality with our ancient meteorologists.

The Sun occupies two-and-one-fourth Nakshatras every month beginning from Aswini, making up 12 months from Aries. It occupies Poorvashadha in the month of Sagittarius and stays there for 13 days and 8 hours (13 degrees and 20 minutes).

If during the 1st day, all the sky including the Sun is found to be completely covered by dark clouds, there will be rain during the month of Gemini when the Sun occupies Aridra.

If during the 2nd day all the heavens are found to be dark with clouds, there will be rain during the latter part of Gemini and the first part of Cancer when the Sun will occupy the asterism of Punarvasu.

On the 3rd day, 4th day, 5th day and 6th day and so on till the 14th day, if the same conditions prevail, there will be rains during the succeeding months when the Sun will be in Pushyami, Aslesha. Makha, Pubba, till Moola in regular succession.

If the *heavens* are clear, then there will be no rain.

Miscellaneous Factors and Rain

Rains can be expected in the following periods also:

(a) When the combustion periods of the various planets begin and end.

(b) On full Moon and new Moon days.

(c) When the Sun transits Cancer and Capricorn.

(d) When the Sun enters the Aridra asterism.

When Mercury conjoins Jupiter or Venus or when Jupiter joins Venus there will be rain.

When Mars and Saturn join planets, then danger from fire, lightning and storms can be expected.

The First Rains and Clouds

We are also enabled to determine the very day of the occurrence of rain from a knowledge of the nature of the clouds during the day. When clouds surrounded by a radiance resembling that of the Moon, with a blue black spot in the centre, and pouring layers of water pass from west to east or east to west, we can predict that there will be very heavy rainfall before long.

Halo at Sunrise shows Rain

If in the rainy season, the sunrise is observed to have a halo in the east and the noon (midday) is marked by the intense heat of the Sun's rays, we can be sure that rain will follow.

Animal Behaviour

Apart from atmospheric factors, the ancient meteorologists also took note of the behaviour of certain animals as indicating immediate rainfall:

(a) Cows hastening home to meet their calves;

(b) Cats scratching the ground with their claws;

(c) Hills shining at a distance with a blue colouring;

(d) The disc of the Moon gets a circular red line, the colour being that of the eyes of the hen;

(e) Chameleons climbing up trees and staring at the sky;

(f) Cows too staring upwards;

(g) Cocks crowing in the day while looking up:

(h) Flashes of lightning are marked in the north-east.

The Moon is observed to have the colour of honey or of the eyes of parrots or doves. The disc of the Moon, though enveloped in clouds, appears to emanate a radiance round in shape or Prathi Chandra (mock Moon).

Immediate rainfall is indicated when:

(a) Claps of thunder crash in the night;

(b) Deep red flashes of lightning are observed during the day:

(c) Cold winds blow from the east;

(d) Young sprouting leaves raise their heads high;

(e) Birds freely bathe in water or in dust;

(f) Serpents bask in the sunshine lying on grass;

(g) Clouds assume the colour of a peacock, parrot. wild crow, or Chathaka bird and take on the shape of waves, hills, tortoise, pigs and fishes.

The Solar Ingress

If the Lagna rising at the time of Aries ingress happens to be a watery sign and is aspected by watery planets there will be proper rains. If the Rasi is a fiery one and is associated with or aspected by fiery planets, there will be no rain.

When Aries ingress happens to fall on Rohini, Anuradha, Jyeshta, Uttarashadha, Abhijit, Sravana, Dhanishta, the year is known as *Indra Mandala*. This kind of year brings on a fear from fire, poverty everywhere, crops fail and autumn crops are destroyed.

When the ingress happens to be on Aswini, Mrigasira, Punarvasu, Uttara, Hasta, Chitta or Swati, then the year is *Vayu Mandala*. Fear from kings, storms and scarcity of rains will be the result.

When the ingress happens to be on Aridra, Aslesha, Moola, Poorvashadha, Satabhisha, Uttarabhadra or

Revati, then the year is *Varuna Mandala*. Good rains and general prosperity will ensue.

If the fifth day of the bright half of the lunar month Chaitra falls: (a) on Monday or Thursday, rainfall will be equally spread throughout the year; (b) if on Wednesday, disturbed rains accompanied by winds; (c) Friday, crops will be destroyed; and (d) Saturday or Tuesday, there will be poor rains.

If the 8th day of the bright half of the lunar month Vaisakha falls on Saturday or Tuesday, famine will set in and the year will be marked by absence of regular rains.

The constellation Mrigasira or Aridra rising on the 1st day of the lunar month, Jyeshta, produces excellent rains.

Weather Changes and Vagaries

Jyeshta Masa Index: The month of Jyeshta (May-June) seems to be very important for measuring the rainfall.

If there is likely to be rain when the Moon passes through certain asterisms from Purvashadha to Moola in the lunar month of Jyeshta, there will also be rain when the Moon passes through the same asterisms in the rainy season.

If there is no rain in the month of Jyeshta, there will be no rain during the monsoons.

If there happens to be a shower during Mrigasira, Chitta, Revati, and Dhanishta in Jyeshta, there will be good rains in the rainy season.

If there is rainfall when the Moon passes through Satabhisha, Jyeshta and Swati, the subsequent rainfall will be ordinary.

Pregnancy of Clouds

The four days commencing from the eighth day in the bright half of the month of Jyeshta (May and June) are known as Vayudharana days. The nature of the health of the pregnancy of the rain clouds can be determined from the winds that blow on these days.

If on the 8th, 9th, 10th and 11th days of the bright half of Jyeshta there happens to be rainfall in the four days when the Moon passes through the asterisms from Swati or Jyeshta, there will be good rains in the rainy season, i.e., from Sravana to Kartika (August to November).

If on the Dharana (rain supporting) days the Sun and the Moon should be covered by wet clouds there will be good rains.

Prospects of Rain—Ashadha Index

Three days in the month of Ashadha (June-July) have been specially selected by our ancient meteorologists for observation of atmospheric conditions with a view to determine the future prospects of rain.

They are the days when in the lunar month of Ashadha, the Moon passes through the asterisms of Rohini, Swati and Uttarashadha. They have been respectively called the Rohini Yoga, Swati Yoga and Ashadhi Yoga days.

Every Hindu astronomer had to study the atmospheric conditions on these three days. If the sky is noticeably covered with huge clouds, serpent-like in shape, white in certain parts and black in certain other parts, or the sky is covered with red clouds or clouds of the colour of blue lotus, and marked by lightning immediately before sunrise and after sunset, this is again a sure indication of heavy rains during the monsoons.

Swati and Ashadhi Yogas

On the Swati Yoga day, rainfall throughout day and night, purports uninterrupted rain for several days in winter.

Wind from the east or north-east on the Ashadhi Yoga indicates good rain, good crops; wind blowing from the south-east, south-west or north-west indicates very little rainfall in the future.

Continuous hot wind from the south-east or high wind from the south-west at sunset, on the Ashadhi Yoga day spells terrible famine.

Rohini Yoga

When the Moon passes through the asterism of Rohini in the dark half of the lunar month Ashadha, Rohini Yoga is caused. The astronomer "shall ascertain the direction of the wind at the time when the Moon enters Rohini. He shall divide this day into eight equal parts (three hours each) commencing from sunrise—the parts representing the eight fortnights of the four months of the rainy season from Sravana to Kartika; and he shall determine on which month or fortnight and how long there will be rain judging from the direction and duration of the wind."

Varahamihira then dwells at length on the nature of the clouds appearing on Rohini day and the results of such appearances.

If on the Rohini Yoga day, the sky is clear and the Sun exceedingly hot, there will be rain in the rainy season. No rains whatsoever and much misery are indicated if unusual phenomena such as meteoric falls, thunderbolts, mock fires etc., occur on the Rohini Yoga day.

Rain Gauging

Rain gauging is also found in astrological texts. According to Varahamihira, falling rain should be collected in a vessel whose capacity is an *adhaka*. An *adhaka* has been defined as the quantity of rainfall which falls to the brim of a vessel 20 inches in diameter and eight inches deep. Four such *adhakas* constitute a *drona*. Equipped with such a rain-gauge our ancient meteorologists were able to measure the exact quantity of rain that fell during the whole season: and by correlating the amount of rain that fell with the factors that made it possible, they were able to predict the exact quantity of rainfall that could be expected in the rainy season. If the 'conception' of clouds is due to all the five conditions of wind, rain, lightning, thunder and clouds, says Varahamihira, then the quantity of subsequent rainfall will be one *drona*, and this will fall over an area of 400 square miles.

If the 'conception' of clouds has been due to wind alone, the resultant rainfall will be three *adhakas*:

If due to lightning, the rain will be nine *adhakas*: If due to thunder, twelve *adhakas*, other factors affecting rainfall.

These quantities of rainfall are, however, modified by the amount of rain that falls on the days when the

Moon passes from the asterism of Poorvashadha to that of Moola in the lunar month of Jyeshta (June-July).

During one month if it rains on the day on which the Moon is in the asterism of either Hasta or Poorvashadha or Mrigasira or Chitta or Revati or Dhanishta then on the corresponding days of the next lunar month, there will be 16 *dronas* of rainfall.

If it rains on days when the Moon is in either Sravana or Makha or Anuradha or Bharani or Moola then on the corresponding days of the next month there would be 14 *dronas* of rainfall. If the Moon resides in either Satabhisha or Jyeshta or Swati, there would be 4 *dronas* of rainfall on the corresponding days of the rainy seasons.

If in Krittika, 10 *dronas;*

If in Poorvaphalguni, 25 *dronas;*

If in Visakha, Uttarashadha, 20 *dronas;* If in Aslesha, 13 *dronas;*

If in Uttarabhadrapada or Uttaraphalguni or Rohini, 25 *dronas;*

If in Aswini, 13 *dronas;*

If in Aridra, 18 *dronas.*

In all the above cases, the subsequent rainfall depends upon the asterisms being unaffected by comets, meteors and the like between the month of Jyeshta and the rainy season.

If the asterisms should suffer by the meeting together in them of the Sun, Saturn and Ketu (Moon's descending node) or by the course of Mars through them or by planetary conjunctions, there will be neither rain nor prosperity in the land.

If benefic planets should pass through the asterisms or if the asterisms should remain unaffected in any of the ways described above, rainfall would be good.

Delivery of Clouds

The delivery or birth takes place 195 days after, when the Moon will be in the same asterism (i.e., seven sidereal months after).

Clouds that conceive in the bright and dark halves of the month of Margasira (November-December) and in the bright half of Pausha (December-January) will be delivered of rain respectively in the dark half of Jyeshta (May-June) and in the bright and dark halves of Ashadha (June-July). But in both these cases the rainfall will only be moderate. Clouds that conceive in the dark half of Pausha will be delivered of rain in the bright half of Sravana (July-August).

Clouds that become pregnant in the bright half of Magha (January-February) will deliver rain in the dark half of Sravana (July-August) and those that become pregnant in the dark half of Magha will deliver in the bright half of Bhadrapada (August-September).

Clouds that conceive in the bright half of Phalguna (February-March) will deliver in the dark half of Bhadrapada and those that conceive in the dark half of Phalguna will deliver in the bright half of Aswiyuja (September-October).

Clouds that conceive in the bright half of Chaitra (March-April) will deliver in the dark half of Aswiyuja and those that conceive in the dark half of Chaitra will deliver in the bright half of Kartika (October-November).

Clouds that conceive in the east will be delivered in the west and *vice-versa*.

Hour of Rainfall

The very hour of the occurrence of rainfall can also be determined; for, says Varahamihira, clouds 'conceiving' during the day will be delivered at night and clouds 'conceiving' at night will be delivered during the day; clouds owing in the twilight of the evening, deliver during the morning. Again, if at the time of conception, clouds have appeared in the east, then at the time of birth, they will appear in the west and so on with the other quarters. Similarly, if at the time of conception the wind has blown from the east, then at the time of rain, it will blow from the opposite quarter.

Clouds that Bring Rain

What are the sums of a healthy 'conception' which would in due course yield abundant rains? For that, the observer must study all atmospheric phenomena, such as rainbows, clouds lightning and thunder from the beginning of the month of Margusira, for about four months. The general atmospheric conditions for a healthy conception of the clouds are as follows:

(a)   Gentle and agreeable winds from the north, northeast and east.

(b)   Clear sky.

(c) Soft, white, deep halo round the Moon or the Sun.

(d) Dark coloured sky, dark as the crow's egg.

(e) Sky overcast with huge bright, dense clouds.

(f) Needle-shaped clouds.

(g) Blood-red clouds.

(h) Rainbow in the morning or in the evening.

(i) Low, rumbling roar of thunder.

(j) Lightning.

(k) The appearance of the mock-Sun; and

(l) Planets shining in full form and with soft light.

Apart from these general signs, certain phenomena observed in certain seasons of the year indicate healthy 'pregnancy' of the rain clouds.

In the month of Margasira (November-December) and Pausha (December-January), red sky in the morning and in the evening, clouds surrounded by halos, and less than usual cold with excessive snowfall are indications of a healthy conception.

In the month of Magha (January-February), the signs of a healthy conception of clouds are high winds, frost and mist obscuring the Sun and the Moon, excessive cold, and sunrise and sunset under clouds.

In the month of Phalguna (February-March) strong, violent winds; fine clouds marching from place to place: broken and imperfect halos round the Sun and the Moon; and the tawny colour of the Sun, all these are indicative of abundant rainfall 195 days later.

Sky marked by winds, clouds and halos in the months of Chaitra (March-April) and Vaisakha (April-May) indicate a healthy conception of clouds.

If during the months of conception (November-May), the pregnant clouds appear to take on the colour of pearls or silver or tamala leaf, or blue lotus, or of collyrium, then the rain during the season will be profuse.

If the pregnant clouds should be exposed to the hot rays of the Sun, or accompanied by gentle winds, then the rain that follows 195 days later will be excessive.

Certain phenomena, however, tend to nullify the chances of future rainfall. Clouds taking the shapes of cities and towers, thunderbolts, dust storms, meteoric falls, appearance of comets in the sky and of spots in the solar disc, occurrence of eclipses—all these are indications that the pregnant clouds will miscarry. Also, if there is heavy rain at the time of conception, or if the symptoms of a healthy pregnancy assigned to the several seasons of the year should fail, then the clouds will yield little or no rain during the rainy season.

Direction of the Wind and its Uses

Here is an experiment suggested in an ancient work to note the direction of wind and its predictive use. Of course in its place we can employ the latest method for observing the direction of the wind.

A thick cloth of 24 feet length and 6 feet width should be hoisted on a pole measuring 144 feet high firmly fixed to the ground, on the morning of the 15th day of the lunar month *Ashadha*. The 'flag' should be carefully observed.

If the flag flies:

(a) towards the east (which means the wind blows from the west) crops thrive well during the year;

(b) towards *agneya* (north-east)—rainfall will be below normal;

(c) towards south or *niruti* (south-west)—clouds form but there will be little or no rain;

(d) towards west— excessive rainfall and strong winds;

(e) towards *vayuvya* (south-east)— enough rains to give good crops;

(f) towards *eeasanya* (south-east)— destruction of crops because of heavy untimely rains.

When the 7th day of the bright half of the lunar month *Ashadha* coincides with the 4th quarter of Purvabhadra, Uttarabhadra or Revati, a clear halo will form around the Sun and the rains will be mixed with heavy winds during the year in question.

Role of Venus

Venus in Hindu meteorology has a close relationship with weather:

(a) Rainfall will be below normal in the year in which, during the lunar months of Sravana, Kartika, Margasira, Magha or Jyeshta, Venus sets and a solar eclipse caused by Rahu occurs.

(b) There will be unprecedented rainfall resulting in heavy floods when Venus rises helically or sets in the constellations of Swati, Visakha and Anuradha.

(c) Famine will break out for want of rains when Venus rises or sets in one of the constellations from Jyeshta to Sravana.

(d) There will be drought conditions when Venus sets in or retrogrades in Makha or Uttarashadha.

(e) When Mars and Saturn are in conjunction, rainfall will be very low.

(f) Clouds become scattered and rainfall disturbed, when the Sun, Mars and Venus transit the same sign.

(g) If Jupiter joins the above combinations, clouds will deliver rains in plenty.

(h) When Jupiter retrogrades in Rohini, the year will have less rainfall.

Much rain results when Jupiter is in Pisces while Venus is in Cancer.

Heavy winds occur when Venus and Jupiter are in any airy triplicity.

Extreme heat is felt when they are in a fiery triangle.

In an Earthy triplicity, the climate is rendered very dry, except when Jupiter is strongly aspected by a moist planet at the time of its ingress into an Earthy triplicity.

When Mars is in Aries in trine to the Sun in Leo, a hot season is made hotter still and warmth added to a cold period. Rain in abundance is shown when they are in a watery triplicity and in conjunction with Venus. Very heavy rainfall follows an eclipse or a great conjunction in Cancer, Scorpio and Pisces and more so if Saturn and Jupiter see each other or they aspect the phenomena referred to.

When the Sun is in conjunction with Sirius, the heat becomes offensive and no rain could be expected unless the Sun is aspected either by Saturn and Jupiter or Venus. When Venus is transiting the area known as Pleiades in Taurus, there is much rain and the air is kept cool.

Snow and Hailstorms

During the cold season Venus in conjunction with Saturn gives rain. In northern and southern latitudes, farther than the Tropic, there will be heavy snowfall. During the hot season, in the equatorial regions, there will be rain and hailstorms.

Mercury in conjunction or opposition with Venus gives both sunshine and showers. Real gloomy weather with heavy mists results when Mercury, Mars and Satum form a Tri-graha Yoga having the aspect of Venus. Cold, dull weather can be foreseen at a time when Saturn is aspected by either the Sun or Mars together with an aspect of Venus

Jupiter in a watery sign in conjunction with or in opposition to Venus gives short showers and a very cool atmosphere. Jupiter so placed with an aspect of Saturn in any airy sign produces a windy and wet day. Plenty of rain follows when Mars in Cancer is aspecting Venus in Libra and the rains will continue for several days if the Moon and Jupiter cast their aspects also.

Mars rules thunder, especially when in a fiery sign it brings terrific thunder without rain. Sometimes lightning also occurs. If aspected either by Venus or Saturn, heavy rains with large drops of water will pour down accompanied by violent thunder.

Whenever the Sun is in conjunction with or in opposition to Saturn the weather is cool (or cold according to the latitude) only if either Mars or Mercury does not aspect the Sun. Similar indications are noted when Jupiter is in conjunction with or in opposition to Saturn.

The aspects of Mars and Saturn produce clear, cool weather with slight showers but Saturn and Venus produce a dull wet time.

Any planet separating from the aspect of Jupiter and applying to an aspect of Saturn reduces the temperature of the air. In latitudes where winter is normal there will be bitter cold winds. Along the equator the temperature will be reduced.

Forecasting the Winter

A mild winter can be easily foreseen when at the time of Sun's ingress into Capricorn (about December 22), the Moon or Venus passes over Saturn and joins Jupiter. A very cold, hard, frosty and snowy winter follows if the movement is from Jupiter to Saturn. This is especially so in countries like England and Germany.

Droughts and Saturn

Droughts are noticed when Saturn is unaspected in Aries, Leo or Sagittarius.

What Kind of Winds

Strong south-west winds are indicated when Mars or Saturn occupy Gemini, Libra or Aquarius and the two are in opposition or square to each other. Mars in Gemini and Saturn in Pisces bring heavy winds.

South-west winds result when Jupiter is in Aquarius in opposition to Saturn in Leo. North-west monsoon winds are ruled by Saturn and south-west, by Jupiter. When they are in airy signs, the direction of the wind is easily ascertained. South-west winds also arise when the eclipse occurs in an airy sign.

Directions: North winds—Jupiter: *Easterly*—Saturn; *Westerly*—Mars; *Southern*—Venus; and *Mixed*—Mercury

The air is essentially ruled by the planet which is applying to the Moon after its conjunction, opposition or square with the Sun.

Constellational Methods to Forecast Rain

Ancient astro-meteorology divides the different constellations into different groups as in the Table below:

Punarvasu, Uttarashadha, Rohini, Jyeshta Uttara, Uttarabhadra, Poorvabhadra, Hasta Anuradha, Abhijit, Pushya, Krittika Satabhisha, Revati, Chitta, Pubba Bharani, Visakha, Aslesha, Sravana Swati, Makha, Dhanishta, Aswini Moola, Purvashadha, Aridra, Mrigasira	Vayunadi Amritanadi Dahananadi Jalanadi Soumyanadi Neeranadi Chandanadi

During winter solstice (Dakshinayana) malefic planets (Saturn, Sun, and Mars) transiting through the Amrita, Jala and Neeranadis, would give rise to ordinary rains. If benefic planets transit the above constellations, there will be plenty of rain.

Planets	Nature of Nadi	Results
Saturn, Sun, Mars	Saumya	Ordinary rain
Jupiter, Venus, Mercury and Moon	Saumya	Good rain
Jupiter, Venus, Mercury and Moon	Vayu, Chanda, Dhana	Ordinary showers
Saturn, Sun, Mars	Vayu, Chanda, Dhana	No rain

Cancer, Pisces and Capricorn are full watery signs; Taurus, Leo and Aquarius are half watery signs; Aries, Libra and Scorpio are quarter watery signs while Gemini, Virgo and Sagittarius are not watery signs.

Aswini, Krittika, Rohini, Purvabhadra, Uttarabhadra, Anuradha, Sravana, Punarvasu, Pushya are masculine; Bharani, Hasta, Chitta, Swati, Visakha, Pubba, Uttara, Aslesha, Makha, Jyeshta,

Aridra, Dhanishta, Purvashadha and Revati are feminine; Satabhisha, Mrigasira and Moola are neutral.

Cast a horoscope for the time at which the Sun enters a certain constellation or a certain quarter of a constellation (in the rainy season). If at this time the Moon is in Jalarasi or watery sign and Mars or Saturn is in the 5th, 7th or 9th from Lagna, there will be heavy rain on that day.

The time (number of *ghatis* after sunrise) at which the Sun enters a particular constellation or quarter of a Nakshatra may be taken as root number; add to this the number of thithi (on the day in question), weekday and the constellation. Multiply the sum by 6 and divide the product by 8. If the remainder be 1, ordinary rain; 2, fairly good rain; 3, ordinary rain; 4, rain accompanied by wind; 5, excess of rain; 6, no rain; and 7, ordinary rain.

In regard to the foretelling of rainfall, (a) the 5th day of the bright half of Chaitra, (b) the 8th day of the light half of Vaisakha, (c) the 1st day of light half of Jyeshta, (d) the lunar months Ashadha and Sravana seem to have some special significance attached to them. Coincidence of certain constellations on certain dates seems to give rise to sudden fall of rain and all these details deserve our careful attention. Of all these, the lunar month Ashadha is of paramount importance according to Varahamihira, which we shall explain at length on a subsequent occasion for the information of our readers.

If the 5th day of the lunar month Chaitra, falls on Monday or Thursday, there will be an equable distribution of rain throughout the year and crops will thrive; Wednesday—disturbed rains accompanied by winds; Friday—destruction of crops; Saturday or Tuesday—want of rains and famine indications.

If the 5th day of Chaitra coincides with the constellation of Aridra, famine conditions during the year are most likely.

If the 8th day of the light half of Vaisakha falls on Saturday or Tuesday—crops will be destroyed for want of regular rains; Monday—plenty; Wednesday—high winds; Thursday—good crops: Sunday—ordinary rains.

If the 1st day of the light half of Jyeshta coincides with the constellations of Mrigasira and Aridra—the rainfall would be plenty; with Bharani, Krittika and Jyeshta want of rain and destruction of crops.

If an assessment on rain has to be made during the monsoon, the best indications are: if the Moon be in one of the watery signs and if that sign at the same time be either the Lagna or the 4th, the 7th or the 10th, it then being the bright half of the month, there will be an abundance of immediate rain; if it be the dark half of the month, and the Moon in one of the watery signs and within sight of benefic planets, there will also be an abundance of immediate rain; if in the latter case, the Moon is aspected by malefics, there will be slight rain.

If the Moon is in the 7th from Venus and within view of benefic planets, or be in the 9th, 5th or 7th house from Saturn there will be immediate rain.

The rainfall would be very great, if the planets are close to the Sun—either towards the east or towards the west.

Practical experience will go a long way towards simplifying these problems; and careful observation will prove that however difficult it may be to unravel some combinations and foresee their precise effects, yet each factor actually exerts its influence and works towards the final resultant.

Of the several methods recommended by classical writers for forecasting rainfall, floods and weather vagaries, the most important ones are: (a) the lunar new year chart, (b) time of pregnancy of clouds, (c) entry of the Sun into the constellation of Aridra, (d) Sun's entry into Capricorn, (e) Rohini, Swati and Ashadha Yogas, and (f) mutual dispositions of planets at a given time.

I shall illustrate some of these methods with reference to the lunar year (17th March, 1961 to 4 March, 1962) which goes under the name of 'Plava'. This means "the land will simply be inundated with water due to heavy rains, people will suffer from affliction and crops will be destroyed by pests". The principal cloud going under the name of *Varuna* takes its origin in the N.W. of Meru, hence indicating heavy rains during the rainy season. It is during the lunar month of Nija Jyeshta (14th June, 1961 to 12th July, 1961) and also in Ashadha (12th July, 1961 to 11th August, 1961) that heavy rainfall and great floods are indicated. In the beginning of the month of Jyeshta, the Sun travels in *dahananadi* for a period of eight days. Venus transits *ativatha* and *vatha* while Mars, Mercury and Saturn progress in *jalamrita soumya rasi nadi*. In the lunar month of Ashadha, the influences are more favourable for causing destructive rains especially because all the planets, excepting

Venus, pass through *rasajalasoumyanadi*. Throughout this lunar month there is no *Ravimadhya dosha*, i.e., the Sun being hemmed in between Mercury and Venus; hence the locus of destruction will be in the western and southern parts. The Sun enters the asterism of Aridra on 20th June, 1961 at about 8.22 a.m. (I.S.T.) (See Chart No. 1).

	Venus		Sun Merc.
Ketu			Ascdt
Jup. (R) Sat. (R)	Chart 1 Rasi		Mars Rahu Moon

Merc. Sat.	Mars	Jup.	Rahu
Saturn			Ascdt
	Navamsa		
Sun Ketu		Moon Venus	Ascdt

The chart is highly significant. The ascendant is Cancer—a profusely watery sign, aspected powerfully by Saturn. Even Capricorn is a semi-watery sign. Hence, Jupiter becomes a watery planet by occupation. Its aspecting Lagna from *amrita nadi*, ruled by the Moon, a watery planet is equally significant.

According to astro-meteorology of the Hindus, the Moon and Venus are full-blown watery planets. Here Venus is situated in the 10th, a powerful place for causing floods. Fortunately here it does not occupy a watery sign but the Navamsa is semi-watery. Mercury is in Aridra itself. These are all influences favouring heavy rainfall. From 1st August to 15th August both the Sun and Mercury will be in Cancer, a *purnajalarasi* while on the 14th and 15th, both the planets will be in *purna jala Navamsa*. About these dates Venus will be in Mesha Navamsa, countering to some extent the indication for heavy rainfall. Added to these, the bright half of the lunar month, Ashadha falls on a Tuesday. According to *PRASNA MARGA*, all such celestial phenomena favour heavy rainfall.

Rain in the Immediate Future

While ancient meteorology can predict rain long in advance, it is no difficult thing to forecast rain in the immediate future.

During the rainy season, immediate rainfall is indicated:

If the Sun at the time of rising is exceptionally bright and red, or

If the taste of water is insipid, or

If the colour of the sky is that of the cow's eye.

If at the time of sunrise or sunset rainbow is seen in the sky, or

If salt begins to sweat, or

If fish in tanks jump from water on the bank, or

If metal vessels emit a fishy smell, or

If ants with their eggs move from one place to another.

When rain is expected and a low cloud is approaching, the odour of metal vessels and of drains becomes noticeable as the lower pressure causes some of the air to escape, and one observes a change in the behaviour of animals and insects which react to a change in the atmospheric conditions. The red colour of the Sun, the halo around the Sun and the Moon and presence of clouds, all indicate the hazy condition of the atmosphere.

Measures can be devised by the authorities concerned to reduce flood-threats by building embankments at vulnerable spots. The intensity of the evil can also be minimised by having recourse to remedial measures prescribed by the sages. These measures consist mainly of employing certain *japas*. It is not superstition that connects *mantras* with rains. *Mantras* are regulated forms of sound vibrations. And sound waves can not only create rainfall but they can also reduce the intensity.

Section 2

Astrology in Earthquake Prediction

Role of Solar Spots

A major earthquake rocked the West Coast of India and razed Koynanagar to the ground at 4.22 a.m. (IST) on 11th December, 1967 causing heavy casualties and rendering thousands of people homeless. Apart from the heavy loss of life and property, the earthquake upset the theory of geologists that the Deccan Plateau was immune to major earthquakes. Considering the intensity of the earthquake, experts felt that the country had indeed escaped with the major havoc confined to a small area. Geologists, geophysicists and seismologists were puzzled as to how this quake could have occurred in a zone which was considered quite safe and busied themselves with making post-mortem studies of the causes. Some Japanese experts who were there, then expressed the view that the major shocks 'were of tectonic origin'. One geophysicist suggested that the impounding of water in the Koyna Dam and the resultant pressures and Earth subsidence, could have caused the earthquake. While conceding the scientist's right to indulge in speculative theories, we have to observe that the catastrophic visitation in this area only demonstrated that Nature has its own unpleasant surprises to reveal, thereby putting human beings in an utterly insignificant stature in the cosmos.

Western scientists think that earthquakes are due to some sudden displacement within the Earth. John Michell, a geology professor of Cambridge University, was the first to attribute the vibratory movement in earthquakes to what he called 'elastic waves traversing the crust.' Though seismology is held to be 'an exact science', we have yet to hear of a seismologist who can predict correctly the occurrence of an earthquake. The only interesting development of seismology seems to be the seismograph which registers even distant earthquakes but of course, only after they have occurred.

On the statistical side (regarding distribution, frequency, secondary effects, periodicity, etc.,) modern scientists have no doubt done considerable research work. The following findings are interesting:

In countries like Italy, Japan, Peru and China, earthquakes are not only of frequent occurrence but of destructive strength also.

In countries like Switzerland, earthquakes are numerous but they seldom cause damage.

According to Mantessu, out of every 100 earthquakes, 53 occurred along the Mediterranean circle, 38 along the circum-Pacific circle and nine, elsewhere. He also supposed that there is an intimate connection between earthquakes and volcanoes. Despite all the advances claimed by seismologists, it is clear that the provision of earthquakes is as yet in its initial stage and that so long as the seismologist confines his investigations only to a study of the 'faults' in the bowels of the Earth, the true causes of earthquakes will continue to remain a mystery.

According to the theory of astrology propounded by ancient sages, all phenomena, including the occurrence of earthquakes, are regulated by planetary movements. Some of the scientists have also been indirectly confirming astrological theories.

For instance, P. Merian noticed that the epoch of greatest frequency occurs in winter, while in insular and peninsular regions, the frequency is greatest in summer.

An exceptionally violent earthquake hit a very densely populated industrial region, 150 kilometres east of Beijing in China in July 1976. The city of Tangshan was reported to be in total ruins. At least 1,00,000 people were said to have lost their lives. The quake-damaged buildings in Beijing, amongst them the famous Hall of the People. Fearing more shocks, the city's six million people stayed out of their houses. The tremors were said to be of a great magnitude damaging several dams, bridges and houses in many parts of north-east China.

Apart from the huge loss of life and property and the need for diversion of resources to rehabilitate the areas damaged, the earthquake in China was also feared to have political implications. The impact of the earthquake on 'superstitious peasants' worried the government, because of the anticipation (of the peasants) that this natural phenomenon 'presaged a national calamity or a change of dynasty', as had been interpreted when monarchs ruled the land.

Scientists, as usual, did not agree as to the exact cause of the earthquakes. Though the Russians claimed about 15 years ago to have made an important discovery in the field of earthquake prediction, nothing further has been known as to whether any reliable system of forecasting earthquakes was developed. Their discovery that the 'ratio between the velocities of natural wave motions through the ground dropped significantly days before an earthquake and then returned to normal just before it took place' is said to be an important step towards the direction of making earthquake forecast. But no two scientists seem to agree either regarding the cause of earthquakes or methods of forecast.

After the Koyna disaster in 1967, the 'water-load' theory was advanced by the French scientist Rothe and later by the Indian scientists, Gupta and Rastogi. Then a team of UNESCO experts found that 'the impounded water was not the cause.' Subsequently Dr. McKenzie of Cambridge and Dr. Brune of California Universities advanced the theory that 'earthquakes lubricate themselves at an early stage and then spread rapidly'.

The astonishing fact is that most of the scientists, engaged in earthquake studies, do not seem to take an integrated view of what is happening on or above the Earth's crust.

It must be noted that it is the planetary positions *vis-a-vis* the Sun that account for earthquakes. Such a theory is not an idle fantasy especially in the light of the findings of some scientists that earthquakes can be triggered by changes in solar activity.

Dr. Anderson, a seismologist of the California Institute of Technology, does not look at seismic events in isolation. In an analysis of a 17-year period of violence (1897 to 1914) "during which there were quakes of a magnitude greater than eight on the Richter scale" he saw that "tsunamis (tidal waves 30 meters' high) increased in number, the length of the day changed, that is, the Earth's rotation slowed down, the world's mean temperature rose by one degree and the 'Chandler wobble was at its peak'." He says further that they were interlinked. All these geo-physical events are part of a large energy-chain. The periodicity of the Chandler-wobble is 40 years and this is said to explain the 1950 and 1952 earthquakes in Assam at Kamchatka.

Therefore, the vagaries of the Sun are not without consequence for our plane, let alone for the human species on it. Dangjon, Director of Observatory at Paris, announced that during January, February and March 1963, the days had been shorter. And it is worthwhile noting that Dangjon announced an important deviation in the Earth's rotation before the disaster of Agadir.

If, as scientists have discovered, the Sun's vagaries alter the duration of the day, it is reasonable to assume that they may even induce earthquakes. In 1966 astronomer Trellis showed evidence that the "gravitational effect of the planets moderates the eleven-year solar-active cycle". Consequently, it is the Sun and the planetary juxtapositions that could afford a mathematically workable method to forecast all natural phenomena including, of course, earthquakes.

The Sun has been worshipped by the great sages of India as a true benefactor. They realised its vast and beneficient influences on the Earth. The Sun which transforms the waters of the ocean into vapour and thus generates the dew, the rain, also the springs, the rivers and organic matter extends his influence to the depths of our planet as well. The Sanskrit classic GARGA SAMHITA traces the quaking of the Earth to Ketus or dark spots on the Sun. This theory is gaining credibility with some modern scientists.

In May 1960 in Chile when everything was shining with joy and freshness, the ground suddenly swung underfoot like an old wooden bridge. Cracks appeared on housewalls. The needles of seismographs jerked and automatic recorders began to pen wild curves. Buildings collapsed like a pack of cards. Thousands were left homeless as Chile was rocked by an earthquake. Two days earlier the scientists had found that a huge spot was passing over the central meridian and they thought that the spot had caused the disaster. And many scientists have also attributed, even if they do not publicly admit this, the formation of solar spots to configurations of planets. It is when the solar spots are large and numerous, that the magnetic storms occur upon the Earth causing in their turn subterranean disturbances, volcanic eruptions etc. Many scientists have been at pains to prove the connection that exists between these terrestrial phenomena and those of the Sun. Indeed it is not the Sun alone which provokes the earthquake shocks. The Moon, the planets and even the comets stimulate the activity of the subterranean forces.

Eleven-Year Cycle Theory

We can construct a simple theory in simple non-technical language. These countless heavenly bodies, as they gravitate round the Sun in turn, approach and move away from it in measured periods, some gravitating alone and others in harmonious groups, some passing rapidly like lightning and in clusters, some slackening their speed when they move away from the Sun as if loath to leave it, some speeding towards it at a headstrong and ever quickening pace.

And all these bodies, which form around the Sun, their common lord, such an animated, harmonious and life-like chain exercise a marked influence upon one another. Infinite in its variety, this reciprocal action depends upon the magnitude of the planets, upon their distance and upon their position in space. The nearer a planet like the Earth is to another planet in the solar system, the more it is attracted by it, and if this planet is powerful, if its action is at any moment combined with that of a neighbouring body to influence the Earth, the latter may be affected to an extraordinary degree. Investigations have been made in view of this, to discover whether at the principal epochs of sidereal influence there have been many severe earthquakes.

More investigations have tended to confirm that a greater proportion of earthquakes falls on the high latitudes at the beginning of the 11-year cycle and on the mean latitudes when the Sun's activity is on the decline. It follows therefore that within a cycle, the centre of seismic activity moves from the high latitudes to the equator. According to some scientists, if we compare the graphs of solar activity, the occurrence of earthquakes and the velocity of the Earth's rotation, we find that the curves are distinctly similar thus showing a definite connection between these three factors.

Decades ago, M. Delanney of France showed that each time the Earth in its revolution round the Sun, is brought within the action of a large planet like Jupiter, there are more or less severe earthquakes. Our own investigations have shown that at the times of severe earthquakes, Jupiter is placed in an angle or the 12th

or 8th from the rising sign at the time of the occurrence of the earthquake.

Jupiter-Rahu Movements

It has also been noted that "shocks are felt more frequently during the quiet hours of the night" shortly after midnight. Milne has also found that great earthquakes are frequent "near the times when changes occur in the direction of the polar movements." It has also been found 'based on the list of destructive earthquakes from 1701 to 1889 recorded in Milne's catalogue' that there are periods of '11, 23, 33, 119 years in earthquakes of the northern hemisphere'. These periodicities remind us of the periodicity of sunspots and, movements of Jupiter and Rahu. At least two scientists—Alekis Perry and Stetson—have come nearer to the truth by indirectly confirming the fact that it is the Earth's relation to the rest of the solar system that is of consequence in predicting earthquakes. Perry asserted that earthquakes are most numerous about the time of new and full Moon, when the Moon is nearest to the Earth and when it crosses the meridian of the place of observation.

According to Dr. H. J. Stetson "When the orbit of the Moon is in a particularly close relation to the epicentres of sources of earthquakes, the strain on the Earth at that point is at its maximum and therefore the crust of the Earth is likely to break producing an earthquake."

It is not only the movements of the Moon that cause earthquakes but other planets, especially Jupiter, which are equally responsible.

Parasara on earthquakes

It is said that the subject of earthquakes has been exhaustively dealt with by Sage Parasara in the third part of his Hora, but unfortunately this particular part has not been traced. We have some notes purporting to be based on this volume, from which it becomes clear that earthquakes are due to some extra-terrestrial causes.

As early as the beginning of Kaliyuga (310 B.C.) Parasara had observed thus: *"Arka Chandra grahana graha vikrithachara jamscha kampana hayulu"*, meaning that when the course of a planet is disturbed from the normal path owing to the attractive forces of other planets, there is a shaking of the planet which is perceived as an earthquake. Though Sage Gargi says that "earthquakes are due to volcanic eruptions", Parasara's view seems to be more reasonable as it can be proved astrologically. In fact, planetary action as an exciting cause of earthquakes is only doubted by those who have never made any fair and complete inquiry into it. Aristotle placed on record the fact that it sometimes happens that there is an earthquake about the time of the eclipse of the Moon.

Site of earthquake

By means of monthly lunations and solar and lunar eclipses, it is possible to predict earthquakes. When a number of superior planets are in conjunction or in the same declination or in the same latitude, there will be earthquakes. Several planets in the Tropics also give rise to this phenomenon. Eclipses falling at quadrants to Jupiter, Saturn or Mars also produce earthquakes.

The area of the occurrence is generally indicated by the zodiacal sign in which the above combinations occur or by the sign which has the conjunction or the eclipse of the meridian or the Nadir. The locality is also indicated in places where Saturn or Jupiter is on the meridian.

		Ascdt	Sun Merc.
Venus			Ketu
Rahu, Sun Moon Mars, Sun Mercury Saturn	Chart 1 Rasi		
		Jupiter	

Ketu			
			Mars
Sun Mercury Moon Venus	Navamsa		Saturn
		Jupiter Venus	Ascdt Rahu

On 15th January, 1934 a massive quake occurred in Bihar. It was a new Moon day and seven planets were in configuration in the sign of Capricom (Chart 1). The Sun, Mars and the Moon were all in exact conjunction in the constellation of Uttarashadha ruled by the Sun, lord of the 8th from the Moon. It will be noted that the earthquake occurred after the Moon entered Capricorn. The occurrence of the earthquake had been forecast by a number of Indian astrologers, long before the event. The sign involved is Earthy. Shocks were also felt in Mexico and Chile ruled by

Capricorn. For China, the deadly conjunction falls in the Nadir. The conjunction and the eclipse have both taken place in Capricorn. Mark the fact that Mercury is in close conjunction with the Moon.

Coming to the July 1976 Chinese earthquake, the U.S. Geological Survey, Colorado, estimated the magnitude of the first quake (which occurred on 28th July, 1976) at 1.15 a.m. (IST) or 3.45 a.m. Peking Time as 8.2 points "on the open-ended Richter Scale" and said that it was the world's strongest for 12 years.

It is said that Chinese scientists had predicted a few weeks earlier of the impending earthquake. According to Dr. C. Barry Raeigh, geo-physicist, and his colleagues in the team that visited China a month earlier, the radio-stations in Peking had been warning the people of the natural calamity. It is also acknowledged that the government could not give any advance warning to the people to stay outdoors.

Ground Glows

One implication of the disaster was the earthquake predicting system could have failed to work. But the American visitors, referred to above, learnt that the Chinese were able to forewarn on the basis of "earthquake lights" or "ground glows" discerned in their laboratories and also by peculiar animal behaviour. Geophysicists say the Chinese theory of "ground glows" is convincing "because of the considerable release of electricity" during the earthquakes, which means a correlation between positions of planets and the electrical disturbances. The American visitors did not wish to dismiss the theory of unusual animal behaviour also. Two hours before the quake, tigers at the Tienstin zoo began acting strangely. There was panic among the chickens. Pigs refused to enter their holes and horses and sheep ran about in a frenzy. Nature's earthquake sensors gave good clues to the oncoming disaster.

In Chart 2, the Lagna is Gemini, an airy sign. There is a five-planet combination in the 2nd house affecting the 8th or house of destruction. Jupiter and Mars are in mutual square (Kendra). The earthquake on the 28th followed in the wake of the new Moon on the 26th. The most important feature is again the closeness of the Moon and Mercury. On the new Moon day, the Moon was in Punarvasu and the earthquake occurred when it entered Aslesha, the constellation held by Mercury. It is evident that the Moon and Mercury have a significant role to play in causing earthquakes.

	Ketu	Jupiter	Ascdt
			Venus Sun Saturn Moon Merc.
	Chart 2 Rasi 28-7-1976		
			Mars
		Rahu	

			Ascdt
Marc. Venus Rahu Jupiter		Navamsa	Mars
Moon			Ketu
	Saturn	Sun Mars	

It will be seen that on the day of the Chinese earthquake except Jupiter (and the shadowy planets Rahu and Ketu) the rest were all clustered within an arc of 38°.

Certain basic astrological facts, bearing on the occurrence of earthquakes, thrust themselves prominently before us after a study of several charts. If, according to modern science, everything in life is electrical in nature, then the tiniest atom and the great cosmos, including the planets, the Earth and the Sun. are therefore subject to certain mathematical laws. We do not know whether earthquakes are caused by gravitational effects of the Sun, the Moon and other planets. The grouping of planets in certain signs shows significant correspondence with earthquakes. Planets may affect the force-field of the Earth and cause earthquakes.

The planetary bodies occupying certain sensitive areas in the zodiac, occasion the occurrence of earthquakes. But the paradox is that though there are astrological principles for predicting earthquakes, some clues are yet to be discovered. There is some snag somewhere and it is only by deep study and research that we can reconstruct astroseismology on the basis of ancient astrological principles.

A careful study of over 200 earthquakes reveals the following interesting features:

(a) earthquakes generally, though not always, occur at the times of eclipses and near new and full Moon days;

(b) The time of occurrence will be near about midnight, midday or early morning;

(c) The major planets—Mars, Saturn, Rahu and Jupiter, and the minor planets—Mercury and the Moon—will be in mutual angles (Kendras) or trines (Trikonas) and near the 10th or 4th house;

(d) The Moon plays an important role and the Nakshatra ruling on that day gives a clue to the area of occurrence on the basis of the *Avakahada* arrangement;

(e) Major planets generally occupy Earthy or airy signs; and

(f) The asterism of the day belongs to "Prithvi" or "Vayu" Mandala.

A study of earthquake charts will confirm these findings.

The most devastating earthquake on the subcontinent of India was the one on 11th October, 1737 at about midnight, when lakhs of people are believed to have perished in the region. On the night between October 11 and 12, a terrible cyclone raged at the mouth of the Ganga. Just as the storm subsided violent shocks of earthquake destroyed innumerable houses not only along the banks of the river but at Calcutta (now Kolkata) also. The waters of the Ganga, it is said, rose more than thirty feet above their ordinary level and more than 300,000 people died. The study of planets on this day reveals that not only were the major planets Saturn and Mars in mutual angles, (Chart 3) but even the meridian and the Ascendant were afflicted. The lunar day was the 3rd.

Moon		Ascdt Saturn
Jupiter Ketu	Chart 3 Rasi	
		Venus Rahu
	Merc.	Mars Sun

	Merc.	Jupiter	Ascdt
	Navamsa		
Moon Saturn			Rahu Sun Mars Venus

Planets in Trikonas

The earthquake of 23rd February, 1887 (time unknown) which caused much destruction in Rivera, Argentina, closely followed the annular eclipse of the Sun on the 22nd of the month. But the Moon (Chart 4) was not in perigee. Mars, Moon and Mercury were in conjunction and in trine to Saturn. Seven bodies are disposed in mutual Trikona Rasis in airy signs.

On 3rd June, 1887 the terrible earthquake of Manila destroyed 1,000 lives. On the 1st June, there was a total lunar eclipse and Moon was in perigee (Chart 5).

Saturn-Mars in Kendras

When an annular eclipse of the Sun took place on 10th November, 1882, the Sun, Moon, Rahu and Mercury

Chart 4 Rasi

Venus			Saturn
Mars Sun Moon Merc. Ketu	Chart 4 Rasi		
			Rahu
		Jupiter	Mars Sun

Navamsa

Moon		Saturn	Rahu Mars Merc.
Sun Jupiter	Navamsa		Venus
Ketu			

Chart 5 Rasi

		Sun Mars Merc.	Saturn
	Chart 5 Rasi		Venus
			Rahu
		Jupiter Moon	

Navamsa

	Mars Rahu		Saturn
Moon	Navamsa		Venus Sun
	Jupiter	Ketu	Merc.

were in Libra and Mars and Saturn in Scorpio and Taurus respectively in mutual Kendras (Chart 6). At the time of the eclipse, Libra was rising in Java. From 13th November began a series of earthquakes which continued at short intervals throughout 1883 'rendering the period memorable for frequency of earthquake shocks and volcanic eruptions.'

	Ketu	Saturn	Jupiter
	Chart 6 Rasi		
Venus	Mars	Moon Rahu Sun Merc.	

	Venus		Rahu
Moon	Navamsa		
Saturn			Mars
Merc. Ketu Jupiter			Sun

Eclipse Degree and Mars

One of the greatest earthquake disasters was the Japanese earthquake on 1st November, 1923. Some 60 per cent of Tokyo alone, including 300,000 houses, was destroyed. 80 per cent of Yokohama was reduced to ashes. The total loss of life was around 140,000. The shocks began just before noon. The ruling star of the day was Bharani presided over by Yama, the deity of destruction (Chart 7). The lunar day was the 6th, neither full Moon nor new Moon. There was a lunar eclipse on 26th August, the eclipse degree being aspected by Mars. At the time of the earthquake, the 10th degree of Scorpio was rising and Mars was exactly in the 10th house and Ketu was in trine from Jupiter.

	Moon				Jupiter	Merc.	Mars
Ketu	Chart 7 Rasi 1-9-1923		Mars Rahu Sun Venus		Navamsa		Sun Sat. Venus
	Ascdt	Jupiter	Saturn Merc.			Rahu	Moon Ascdt

New Moon and Mutual Kendras

When the Bihar earthquake took place on 15th January, 1934, it was a new Moon day (Chart 1). Except Venus all the planets were in mutual Kendras, the Moon and Mercury being in exact conjunction and the sign involved being watery. The constellation is Uttarashadha and the earthquake occurred after the entry of the Moon into Capricorn. Mercury and Jupiter, the indicators respectively of knowledge and wisdom in natal Astrology, cannot escape the blame for causing earthquakes. Mercury is unstable, and therefore, possibly reflects the vibrations of other planets.

Jupiter-Saturn Opposition

The Assam earthquake which occurred on 15th August. 1950 is said to be the greatest recorded up to this time, and British observers calculated that "Mount Everest had been lifted two feet by it". Here again the earthquake occurred just two days after new Moon when the Moon was near perigee (Chart 8). Mars and Jupiter are in mutual trines while Mercury was in conjunction with both the Moon and Saturn. Jupiter and Saturn are in opposite signs. Another factor to be noted is the situation of Mars and Jupiter in airy signs.

Ascdt Rahu				Ketu	Sun		
Jupiter			Venus				
	Chart 8 Rasi 15-8-1950		Saturn Moon Merc. Sun	Jupiter Mars	Navamsa		
		Mars	Ketu	Merc. Saturn	Moon	Ascdt	Rahu Venus

Jupiter-Saturn Conjunction

Two of the worst earthquakes occurred in 1960 perhaps due to Jupiter-Saturn remaining in the same sign.

earthquakes uprooted the coastal city of Agadir, in France leaving over 12,000 dead. The first quake hit the town just before midnight on 29th February, 1960.

How severe the tremors were can be judged from the fact that the earthquake was registered by seismographs as far away as in Moscow and even the recording instruments in Morocco were damaged by the shock. According to Professor Bernal, the energy required for such an upheaval would approximate the strength of one thousand hydrogen bombs. Immediately after the first tremor, a huge tidal wave swept in adding enormously to the suffering of the people. Floods, fires and sea erosions all followed the disastrous earthquakes.

The Moon rules liquids and hence in the occurrence of earthquakes, it has a significant part to play. It will be seen that the earthquake on the 29th February (Chart 9) followed the new Moon on the 26th in Aquarius, an airy sign. On 27th the Moon joined Mercury and on the 29th the Moon was exactly in a Kendra from Saturn. The disposition of Rahu, Saturn and Jupiter, and the Moon and Mercury in mutual Kendras is also to be noted. The asterism was Revati, ruled by Mercury.

About three thousand people were killed and 3,000 injured in the earthquake which shattered the south Persian towns of Ler and Carash on 25th April, 1960. The first shock occurred at 13 G.M.T. It cannot

Moon Merc. Ketu			
Sun	Chart 9 Rasi 29-2-1960		
Mars Venus			
Saturn Jupiter		Ascdt	Rahu

Moon Sun		Ascdt Mars	Jupiter Venus
Rahu	Navamsa		
			Merc. Ketu
	Saturn		

be a coincidence that on 23rd April, the Moon occulted Mercury and passed through Kendra positions from Jupiter and Saturn. It was a new Moon day. The Ascendant is an Earthy sign, aspected by Mars (Chart 10). Both Jupiter and Saturn were near the lower meridian while Mercury was setting. Jupiter, Saturn, Mercury and Rahu were all in mutual Kendras, the Nakshatra being that of Ketu.

A most terrible earthquake disaster devastated several thousand square miles of northwest Iran on 2nd September, 1962, the first shock having occurred at 10.55 p.m. It brought ruin to 75 towns and villages and according to official reports, ten thousand people were killed.

The Lagna is again an Earthy sign, Taurus (Chart 11). The earthquake followed in the wake of the new Moon on 30th August, 1962. The most remarkable

Chart 10 Rasi 25-4-1960

Venus Ketu Mercury	Sun Moon		
Mars			
Jupiter Saturn			Rahu Ascdt

Navamsa

Venus		Mars Ascdt	Moon
			Jupiter Ketu
Rahu Merc.			Sun
	Saturn		

Chart 11 Rasi 2-9-1962

		Ascdt	Mars
Jupiter			Rahu
Ketu Saturn			Sun
		Venus	Moon Merc.

Navamsa

		Ketu Merc. Saturn	
Jupiter Mars			Ascdt
	Venus Rahu		Sun Moon

feature is again the fact that the Moon passed over Mercury on 1st September having trined Saturn also. Jupiter was exactly in the 10th house, though not in the *medium coeli*, and Mars and Jupiter in mutual trines. Mercury and Mars were again in mutual Kendras.

Historic Fact

One of the greatest of all known earthquakes was that which ruined Lisbon on 1st November, 1755. It is reported that shocks were felt all over Portugal and parts of Spain, southern France and northern Africa totalling the disturbed area to nearly a million square miles. "The sea retired, laying bare the bar and then rolled into a height of 40 feet. In Italy and Switzerland lakes were set in oscillation". The destruction of life was immense. It will be seen that on the day of the earthquake Mars, Jupiter, Rahu and Moon were in mutual Kendras. Saturn and Jupiter were in Earthy signs, and the earthquake occurred two days before new Moon (Chart 12). The day of the earthquake was 1st November. Marie Antionette was born on the 2nd November, 1755, under almost the same turbulent pattern of the heavens. Her fateful life and how she died is self-explanatory.

For years, we had been in correspondence with the nuclear physicist Dr. Tomascheck (See Appendix). According to him the grouping or 'picture' of the planets about certain axes shows significant correspondence with earthquakes. A 'gestalt' factor is present. It has been found that Jupiter is associated with the strongest of earthquakes in contrast to its astrological significance in human relationships.

			Mars	Sun Moon	Venus		Mars Ketu Jup.
Ketu				Saturn			
	Chart 12 Rasi 1-11-1755				Navamsa		
Saturn			Rahu				
	Merc.	Sun Venus	Moon Jupiter	Rahu		Merc.	

In my editorial dated 14th November, 1977 appearing in *The Astrological Magazine*, the January 1978 issue, I predicted: "There will be a total lunar eclipse on Saturday, 16th September, 1978, involving the Virgo-Pisces axis. There is a possibility of a major earthquake also, about the area of Iran." The newspapers of 18th September, 1978, carried headlines of the earthquake in Iran which killed over 10,000 people. The earthquake occurred on the night of 16/17th September, 1978, resulting in a huge loss of life and property.

The disaster occurred just after full Moon (Chart 13), an eclipse of the Moon had occurred. Jupiter and Mars were in square while the waxing Moon had just passed through an exact opposition with Mercury, the previous day.

Ketu Moon			
	Chart 13 Rasi 16-9-1978		Jupiter
			Saturn Merc.
		Mars Venus	Sun Rahu

Saturn			Moon
Sun	Navamsa		Saturn Ketu
	Mars		Merc. Jup.

In an editorial written on 15th November, 1989, which appeared in *The Astrological Magazine*, January 1991, I wrote: "Rahu, situated in Capricorn 24° 45' (Dhanishta constellation) at the beginning of the English year enters Sagittarius on 25th April, 1991, having conjoined Saturn on 21st January, 1991 in Capricorn 7° in the constellation of Uttarashadha. The implication of this particular conjunction in regard to world affairs will be discussed on a subsequent occasion. Jupiter-Mars opposition (1st February, 1990), Saturn-Mars conjunction (28th February, 1990) and Jupiter-Saturn opposition (14th July, 1990) are capable of triggering earthquakes in earthquake-prone areas like Iran, Assam, China and Mexico, especially about the times of the new Moon and full Moon." Exactly as anticipated a massive earthquake rocked Iran on 21st June, 1990. The earthquake occurred on a Chaturdasi (Chart 14), just before new Moon. Mercury conjoined

Moon on 21ˢᵗ June, 1990. The major planets Mars and Jupiter were in square.

Mars		Moon Merc. Venus	Sun Jupiter
	Chart 14 Rasi 21-6-1990		Ketu
Rahu			

	Mars	Jup.	Rahu
	Navamsa		
Venus Mars Saturn			Mercury
	Sun Ketu		

In October, 1989, earthquakes occurred in Los Angeles and China. I had indicated these quakes in *The Astrological Magazine*, Annual (January) 1989 issue, while discussing the trends for the year 1989: "Unusual weather conditions in certain states may cause loss of life and damage to property. An earthquake is possible in California about August-September." The quake occurred in October 1989 which in seismological terms is remarkably correct, especially because of the fact that the return periods of large seismic events are of the order of few decades according to Dr. Arun Bapat of the CWPRS, Khadakwasla, Pune, who wrote to me congratulating me on this accurate prediction. In the same editorial under "China and the Far East," I wrote "A major natural disaster such as an earthquake is likely somewhere near the province of Sinkiang about the time of the Jupiter-Saturn opposition." The opposition took place on 9th September, 1989 and the quake hit China in October, 1989.

These predictions were based on astrological factors. I would like to ask which seismologist in the whole history of seismology, not only in our country but anywhere in the world, came close to making such a prediction in spite of all the resources and funds being spent on this science. Yet a giant inferiority complex tightly holds back our thinkers from looking at the remarkable methods of earthquake forecasts which astrology offers. It is the tragedy of our times that our government would rather see thousands and tens of thousands of people die than take recourse to astrology. Nothing can be more ironic than the fact that in the country of its own origin, astrology is not recognised for its true worth.

There is no doubt that the causes of earthquakes lie outside the relationships that natural physical science deals with today. The planetary groupings can release the accumulated energy resulting in a quake. As Mr. Gulomanoy says: "The energy of the tectonic processes is very great. Imagine that tension appears and energy begins to accumulate in some region of the Earth. In the long run a moment comes when little is needed for an earthquake to begin. An earthquake may be triggered by changes in solar activity."

Scientists should note that our Earth, apart from being an inert mass, is also a living organism and that it is sensitive to the Sun's rhythms. If only our Universities and National Laboratories devote at least a meagre part of their talents and resources to astroseismology, they can discover simple mathematical methods based on ancient astrological guidelines which will enable them to forecast the occurrence of earthquakes and other similar natural catastrophes so that precautions could be taken in advance to minimise human suffering.

If only modern scientists could keep their minds open, the accumulated wisdom of Astrology could be of great assistance.

The loss of life and damage to property are the chief features of a great earthquake. The death toll rises appallingly in a matter of minutes. While we cannot prevent this natural phenomenon, we can certainly endeavour to lessen the destruction by heeding the forecasts.

earthquakes occur because of the disturbances of Earth's field-force. And these disturbances are brought about by the incessant motion of planets.

Appendix

A Great Physicist Becomes an Astrologer

Sir, I was very glad to receive your kind letter dated 30th September, 1948, and I thank you very much for sending me some past issues of *The Astrological Magazine*, which made a very interesting reading for me.

I am sorry for the delay in replying but work at the laboratory has kept me from it.

Perhaps, you are interested in knowing how a physicist has turned to astrology. As you see from my date of birth, it is at least according to the western astrology, quite understandable. I am born on 23rd December, 1895, Oh, 46m. p.m. G.T. = 1h. 44m. I.T. 49° O' N, 14° 29' E. Uranus exactly on the descendant seems quite significant. It seems to me more a map for inner development than for outer success.

As all western scientists of my age, I ignored and despised astrology, embraced by the materialism of my time and my surroundings. But a strong philosophical training and inclination prevented me from accepting this materialism as the true way of science. I never lost the conviction that there must be a spiritual ground to all physical happening.

The time was ripe when Pluto was transited by Uranus. This brought on the exact day a fundamental change in my outer life. The following transit of Uranus over Neptune led me to the knowledge of astrology and its appreciation. It was the coincidence of planetary constellations and the events which they indicate according to the astrological teaching, which convinced me. Especially one occurrence gave the starting point to my thoughts. It was the following: I met—as a cause of the events of war—a colleague of mine who with his institute had moved from Vienna into the village as I had done from Munich and in the course of events, we joined with our institutes in the same house. I was very surprised to learn that he was born exactly the same day as I was, not far away (about 50 miles). We were both physicists; both Directors of big Institutes and worked in similar, but, not exactly the same fields. This event at this time more received in the subconscious—later became the starting point of my conversion as it were.

I must confess that astrology has given me an immense widening of inner horizon and I think it is one of the most important means to overcome materialism.

You will perhaps be surprised to hear, that though my whole life has been devoted to discover the electro-magnetic structure of matter and the atoms, yet I refuse to explain the astrological effects of the planets by an electromagnetic action. I think that the planets in their orbits and the man in his life are parts of one infinite happening where all is linked together by one breathing principle.

As to the outer events of my life, it may perhaps interest you in connection with my map, that I lost my father at six years of age. Nearly at the same time I lost more and more my eyesight in my right eye (which must have been disturbed already at birth), at ten (or 11 years) I underwent an operation of this eye and the lens was extracted. I am now blind in this eye, astrologically quite understandable. In 1918 I married and divorced in 1927. In this year, I was married the second time (Uranus, Mars). In the same year I became Assistant Professor, 1934 and Director of the Institute of Physics at Dresden, 1939 at Munich. I have written several books (a textbook in German now has 14 editions), in English 4 reprints and 18 translated into Spanish and edited about 70 scientific papers. 1945, I lost my position in consequence of the marching-in of the Americans. It clipped severely my material resources, but gave me the possibility of studying astrology without any other disturbance. Rahu conjunct Ascendant brought me new material possibilities here in England.

I should be very glad to hear from you again.

Surrey, England   **R. Tomaschek, Ph.D.**